Charles Edward Buckingham

The Proper Treatment of Children

medical or medicinal - being the annual discourse before the

Massachusetts Medical Society, June 4, 1873

Charles Edward Buckingham

The Proper Treatment of Children
medical or medicinal - being the annual discourse before the Massachusetts Medical Society, June 4, 1873

ISBN/EAN: 9783337816346

Printed in Europe, USA, Canada, Australia, Japan

Cover: Foto ©Andreas Hilbeck / pixelio.de

More available books at **www.hansebooks.com**

THE PROPER TREATMENT OF CHILDREN.

BY CHARLES E. BUCKINGHAM, M.D.

OF BOSTON.

Read at the Annual Meeting of the MASSACHUSETTS MEDICAL SOCIETY, June 4, 1873.*

MR. PRESIDENT AND FELLOWS
OF THE MASSACHUSETTS MEDICAL SOCIETY:—

THE Massachusetts Medical Society has, it is said, been on trial for the past year or more, for the purpose of discovering if it had the legal right to manage its own affairs. The Supreme Court of the State has been sitting upon the question; and, while waiting for its decision, the Committee of our body has wisely allowed all discussion of the subject quietly to rest. And now that the question has been decided, and all noisy declamation has been avoided, it may be as well for us to review the history of our Association, and look somewhat into its real object and its relations to the public, by whom and for whom it exists.

---

* At an Adjourned Meeting of the Mass. Medical Society, held Oct. 3, 1860, it was

Resolved, " That the Massachusetts Medical Society hereby declares that it does not consider itself as having endorsed or censured the opinions in former published Annual Discourses, nor will it hold itself responsible for any opinions or sentiments advanced in any future similar discourses."

Resolved, " That the Committee on Publication be directed to print a statement to that effect at the commencement of each Annual Discourse which may hereafter be published."

1

It exists by virtue of an act of the Commonwealth, not for the privilege of money making, not for the purpose of giving one set of men power over others, not to enable the so-called regular practitioner to take an advanced position at Court or on State occasions; but, in the words of its charter, "As health is essentially necessary to the happiness of society, and as its preservation or recovery is closely connected with the knowledge of animal economy, and of the properties and effects of medicines; and as the benefit of medical institutions formed on liberal principles, and encouraged by the patronage of the law is universally acknowledged;— Be it therefore enacted," &c.

We can easily imagine how much more professional jealousy existed among men equally well educated, before the year 1781, when this charter was granted; and how much this may have done to bring together, at that time, and to make known to each other the men of ability, of knowledge, yes, and of honesty in their practice, who had hitherto kept aloof from each other.

In 1781, the profession and the public of New England were not so well off, so far as professional knowledge is concerned, as they are to-day in the farthest settlement of the most newly settled territory.

There were, it is true, men who had been educated abroad, and who, for family reasons, the desire for excitement, or on account of bad habits and worse name, had settled in the colony; and some of them were undoubtedly well educated for the time.

But the great mass of medical practitioners had passed no examination, and received no degree. A few of them had pored over the small number of well-thumbed books in some equally unexamined doctor's office; but ignorance of books, was the rule.*

The most plausible talker, the sweetest smiler at the lady's couch, the hypocritical knave who anxious-ly sought opportunity to pray himself into practice at the bedside of the dying ; these were the men who most rapidly, if not permanently, came into lucrative practice. The custom is not yet abolished ; but with the growth of knowledge, and the more free intercourse of men of education, the evil has become comparatively slight.

At this day, attempts are made, by those who mean well, to make one standard of medical educa-tion, a requirement throughout this whole land, or to refuse fellowship to those who are not up to it. That standard cannot be forced, beyond the require-ments of the situation, by this Society, nor by the American Medical Association.

The same amount of education is not needed in some little settlement in Omaha, that must be had in a large city. To get an equally well educated man for such a place, would require more money than the whole settlement could furnish, and the re-sult would be, that it would be without any medical attendant whatever. Nor in this Commonwealth is an equally well informed medical man required in every village, nor could such afford to live there.

---

* Note A.

The Society was intended to protect the public, and to distinguish from pretenders, those who believe in no dogma, but who wish to practise honorably according to the light received. It asks no man whether he believes in bleeding or aconite as more certain to relieve fever; whether he knows that capsicum will cure sore throat or a cold bath be followed by sweating; whether belladonna will prevent scarlatina or nux vomica will stop tetanus; whether he intends to use any particular drug in the treatment of any particular disease, nor whether he believes that every patient will do better without any medical treatment than with it.

Notwithstanding the precedence which, under some circumstances, is awarded to knaves; it is on the whole true, that by the existence of this Society, the better men are more patiently listened to. Hardly a man of us, who has been in court, but knows how testimony of honest men is twisted against themselves; and how, after they have left the room disgusted with the jury, the bench and the bar, they have cursed law as a dishonest trade, and those who practise it as but little better than practical traders. But physicians must remember the difficulty in appreciating the mote in the eye, unless it gives pain to the bearer. Let them look around upon their own brothers, and they find the same trickiness in every profession; theology, law, medicine. And the day comes when the best man in his calling is the man sought for. Enough has been had of the professed professional witness; but now the services of him, who is known to be looked up to by his professional brethren, are required, and the best man among regular practitioners is called for; not necessarily the man whom the public have supported the most, but the one whose opinions you and I respect.

There are those who sorrow because the profession is looked upon with less of adoration than in former years; and so it is with the pulpit. We are not alchymists. We have no secret cures. There are those among us who doubt if we have any cures, and yet practise medicine with perfect success and honor.

We should cheer all such on, if we believe in " the benefit of medical institutions formed on liberal principles and encouraged by the patronage of the law." In one thing we all agree; and that is, in ignoring theories unsupported by facts. We require to-day the evidence of any man's claim to a successful treatment of any disease, if he speaks of such; and as members of this body, we are willing and anxious to hear from those who have had experience, whether we agree with them or not. We believe it to be a matter of duty, for those who have reached a certain position, to give the results of their observation to those who are coming after; and this, notwithstanding the certainty that the observations of different men do not and cannot agree. It remains for some other party to point out the reasons for the discrepancy, and to draw the proper conclusions. It is simply an absurdity, to bind ourselves by any one set of observations; for no two cases can be alike in all their present surroundings and all their precedent history. Those who are so easily satisfied that they are right, from the fortunate result of single cases treated by them, it would be wasted time to talk to. We too often hear of the many hundreds of cases of some one disease, treated by a single man, when his whole constituency must necessarily have been afflicted with it, to enable him to count a tithe of the number.

I remember well in the early years of practice, and there are others present who cannot have forgotten it, the having commented with severity, at a society meeting, upon the injudicious treatment of scarlet fever by those who reported the cases. We were, most of us, dispensary practitioners. Their patients died; my patients got well. But what did their percentage or mine in the grand result amount to? Absolutely to nothing.

The surroundings of dispensary patients differ as much as those of patients in higher life. Every patient was not lying over a sewer. Every patient did not have a tuberculous ancestry. Every patient was not properly clothed, nor every one badly fed, nor every one injudiciously dosed by some dangerous neighbor. But the tables turned and percentages changed. Called to a child on Saturday afternoon, I found it one of five children in an Anglo-American family, just taken down with scarlet fever. The other four, so far as I could judge, were in perfect health. Before Monday night the five children were buried.

" But of what use is it," asked a member of the profession, " to tell stories like this to the public, or even to the profession? It will only cause distrust of our remedies, and want of confidence in ourselves. The profession is sufficiently split up by differences of opinion in matters of treatment now."

And because of these differences of opinion concerning treatment I am glad. It shows thought, at least on the part of some. The public are not capable of judging. The same is true of many of the profession. The illogical exist within as well as without its doors. Discussion, however, and fair, candid statement of facts, will not deprive the profession of its proper standing. Indeed, a properly recorded set of observations, properly discussed by those who are looking for true conclusions, never injured the reporter nor the profession. And if the profession is to be destroyed by absolute " knowledge of the animal economy and of the properties and effects of medicines"; why, gentlemen, the sooner it dies, the better; that we may earn an honest living by the sweat of the brow. It cannot be so, however. Prove, to-day, that *medicinal* treatment of any one disease, is useless or harmful, the *medical* treatment still remains for us; and instead of wasting thought, poring over old books to enable us to decide upon medicinal combinations, we have the time before us for the study of the causes of the disease, and its prevention and even its cure. Medicine is not the only curative means; and were medicines (I do not say medical treatment) proved to-day to be absolutely useless or even noxious, there would still be enough for the physician to do.

The relation of men to each other is such, that it has been found not only convenient, but necessary, to set certain men apart for certain work. All have not time to hew timber, nor to lay brick. All have not the peculiar mental capacity to learn mathematics and navigation, nor the physical power to dig the ditch; and to some of us has been left the teaching of anatomy and surgery, of the mechanism of labor, of the physiology of digestion, of the easiest method of nursing, yes, even of the preparation of gruels, and the administration of enemata.

Less than fifty years ago, almost every thinking man knew that the railroad system, if allowed to exist, would destroy the trade in horses, would throw hundreds of men out of employ who were engaged in stage building and driving, and would even oblige the poor farmer to sit with folded hands and starve, because there would be no use for his hay and his grain. But progress in railroad building has brought forward other problems to be solved. Where are we to get all the material that is going to be needed to supply the roads with cars? The wood has been cut off, and it has become necessary to supply coal for fuel in its place, or cars will not run. As the coal is used, why not be alarmed lest that should be burned up and even Pennsylvania be left without means to afford us warmth and motion? My brethren, the progress of knowledge, consequent upon accident some may say, but surely consequent upon study and thought, consequent upon the intercourse between men of the same trade or profession, consequent upon discussion which sometimes seems severe, has always made the want and the supply come together, like the hour and the man.*

* Note B.

It is useless for us to cling to the old, one moment after it is proved valueless. It is useless, one moment, to try and retain that which will not do the work so well as something else. He who waits is lost.

You may respect the knowledge of him who stood at the head of his profession fifty years ago, or some of you may laugh at his ignorance. But if Sydenham were here to-day, if Galen were a member of this Society, their position would still be in the front rank. They would not be

> "The first by whom the new are tried;
> Nor yet the last to lay the old aside."

We say, as a Society, nothing against proper medicinal treatment; we only ask for properly recorded histories and results to prove its propriety. But we want the whole history, the liberty to ask proper questions, and the power of full investigation. If we find our results not what we expect as logical conclusions from our premises, we are not such fools as to refuse further examination. If we find that we have neglected that which our fathers taught of what they thought they knew, we may, it is true, go back to venesection. Though I do not believe that what we knew as antiphlogistic treatment, will ever be revived; yet I can imagine the case in which the lancet may be needed, or in which the actual cautery may seem to be the only resort.

The relations of this Society to the public are such, " because health is essentially necessary to the happiness of society," that, as a profession, we are bound to investigate the minutest point and to

2

acknowledge the slighest error. There is no reason why quackery should exist among us; and by the freest examinations, and the most candid acknowledgment of errors, quackery is the most easily to be disposed of.

In 1849, some of us who were attached to the Cholera Hospital in this city, were asked what objections we could make to allowing homœopaths to have charge of the hospital with us. We made no objection. We simply proposed, that the patients should be put in alternate beds for their treatment and ours, as they came in; that we should have the right to examine each other's medicines, and see that the treatment was what it purported to be. But our proposal was rejected, and the hospital remained in the hands of those first appointed. Investigation is a necessity with us; and, as before intimated, if properly conducted, it can do no harm.

There is no reason why we should not listen to new facts. Indeed, we cannot help listening to them. There was a time when the raising of certain fruits was a pleasure and a profit to the farmer. On riding through the State, to-day, one is somewhat struck with the fact that a large number of apple orchards have been suffered to go to decay; and, upon inquiry, he is informed that the tree is so fearfully diseased, that the farmer believes it will cost him more than he can receive in return, to take care of it. He turns his attention, therefore, to his pigs and cows, sheep and horses. If he believed that the cost of these animals would not be returned to him with interest, it would soon be seen that, like apple trees, they would be neglected and suffered to die, or even that active warfare upon them would be begun, only to end with their extermination. If the farmer knew that one-fourth part of his stock must die of disease before its first infancy was passed, would it not be difficult to persuade him to raise stock any more? If by discussion with other men of his own profession, he could find out the causes of his loss, he would no longer hesitate, whether the result was to be in cider or in colts. And does this apply to medical men? Certainly, to all men. And no investigation, properly conducted, can do harm. You can no more force mankind to take physic, unless you can make them think there is reason for it, than you can oblige them to burn tallow candles or cultivate apples.* And if there be those who know that to prolong life you must "purge freely," so there are those who believe that the world is not so well off as it was when the distinction between classes was greater; who believe that master and serf was a good condition: but you also will find that some of them only believe these things, in case they were themselves to be masters; or, in the other case, if through some one else were to be the channel for the Elixir Pro.

To our Society, in this Commonwealth, belongs the investigation of the facts upon all matters of health, whether hygienic or therapeutic.

The abusive name of Allopath has been put upon regular practitioners by those who pretend to

* The writer does not forget that the fears of some people may be so acted upon to-day, that they will take whatever is recommended, when sick. He is looking forward to the results of medical investigation.

believe in what they call Homœopathy, and some
of our number have been willing, thoughtlessly, to
receive it.   But every man belongs to the army of
quacks who allows, for one moment, a system.   The
moment you acknowledge, as a foundation for treatment, any dogma whatsoever, that moment you are
among those who profess to cure diseases by Spirit-
ualism, Homœopathy, or Thomsonism.   That moment you are attempting " to disorganize or destroy
the Society."   That moment you have commenced a
warfare against investigation and progress; and
although your position may be a pecuniary success,
and although it may not be possible to rid the Society
of your presence, it would " be disreputable for any
Fellow to advise or consult" with you, or in any way
to abet or assist you as a practitioner of medicine or
surgery.

Allow that medicinal treatment should be proved
useless, which no man among us believes; would
there be nothing left for the physician to do?

The population of Massachusetts, at the time of
taking the last census, 1870, was 1,457,351.   There
were born of living children, in the years 1865 to
1870, 209,989.   There died in the same years, of
children under three years of age, 47,671; and of
these 31,326 were less than one year old.   There
were living in 1870, 95,346 children under three
years of age.   That is to say, that in those six
years, there died of children under three years old,
only two less than one-half of the number living in
1870; and of these more than six-tenths died at the
age of less than one year.   Why this mortality? is a

subject for us to investigate. And this is but one
question. And this leads to another, and a third,
indefinitely. And so does every other question
which may come up. It was merely selected as one
subject for illustration. Let us pursue it for one
moment. Why should there be so large a mortality
among human beings in infancy, compared with the
mortality among domestic animals? There are
several causes, some of which may be avoided, and
some of which neither law nor argument can
overcome.

The farmer and stock raiser are cautious in select-
ing the originals from which cows and pigs and sheep
are to be raised. The bounds of fences and stable
walls are a safeguard against the propagation of
diseased animals, which the stock cannot overcome.
The love which laughs at locksmiths among human
stock, cannot easily overcome the bolts and bars of
Eclipse's residence and the bed-chamber of the fair
Goldsmith Maid.

And we never shall and never ought to reach that
condition of society when parentage shall be established by law, and when certain families shall be
forced to die out, because a grandmother had phthisis
or her father was suspected of syphilis. The marriage of convenience is more likely to be followed
by mental and physical suffering and moral decay
than the marriage induced by love. If the children
of the latter are not born in every respect faultless,
so far as health is concerned, there certainly may be
much done to improve their faulty condition. Were
it possible to prescribe the particular husband and

the particular wife, the result, in form of child, would be more difficult to determine than now, when parties are left to make their own selection. The certificates concerning result would be like the certificates attached to other quack prescriptions of the day; and you would find it difficult to say if directions had been implicitly obeyed.

A word in behalf of children at this point.

Some years ago, while in attendance upon a veterinary surgeon of some note, who has since died, I asked him how he found out what was the matter with a horse, and how he detected his disease. His answer was: "How do you find out what is the matter with a sick baby? Babies and horses don't lie."

And I imagine, if patients, generally, were unable by their own foregone conclusions as to their diseases, and by questions and answers framed upon these conclusions, to deceive their thinking medical attendants, involuntary though the deception often be, that their sickness would be often less, and the time of our attendance shortened.

Of 9,873 children who died in Massachusetts in 1870, under the age of five years, 1914 were reported as by cholera infantum, 477 by convulsion, 298 by diarrhœa, 273 by dysentery, 110 by enteritis, 495 were called infantile, 166 by canker, 2 by starvation, 302 by tabes mesenterica, 308 by teething. Leaving out the 610 deaths by cause reported unknown, and 366 by hydrocephalus, more than three-fourths of all reported as from those causes; considering what we know of the causes of convulsion, diarrhœa, dysentery, &c., it cannot be unfair to infer, that at least one-half of all these deaths were caused or consequent upon diseased digestive organs. That is to say, that of the 9,873 deaths of young children, more than one-half were from diseased digestive organs. It is the misfortune of the human species, that they are not endowed from birth with the power of distinguishing good from evil in their food. You can spoon death into their stomachs from the hour of cutting the umbilical cord. There the baby of the lower animal has the advantage. He is fed on natural food, only, from the beginning, because his father and mother don't know enough to kill him. Man, the reasoning being, is defeated by the animals, who possess instinct only. They never for amusement, nor curiosity, experiment upon the stomachs and lives of their children, with the desire of seeing how much indigestion they will bear with impunity. I am not alone in the belief that the excessive mortality, at an early period of infancy, is, very much of it, caused by attempts to substitute for natural nourishment that which will save time and trouble to the mother, and by attempts to force growth.

Why do American born females make such poor wet nurses compared with the immigrant from Ireland or Germany? After nearly thirty years of practice I cannot answer the question. That it is the fact, few practitioners in our large towns and cities doubt. Allow that some women, with us as with foreigners, object to be bound to their children's calls, yet the mass of American females are totally unable to act the wet nurse with success. The consequence of the early failure of the supply is the early attempt to fit the stomach for other food. Add to this the parental pride which interferes for the poor pleasure of seeing a toothless child swallow the food of an adult, and you have for the result — cholera infantum, dysentery, convulsions, tabes mesenterica, and if, by reason of extra strength, the child passes the first dentition, it is more likely to be cut off during the second, or to become later a dyspeptic, or even phthisical.

Dr. Cumming, of Atlanta, Ga., wrote a little unpretending but useful tract, some years ago, upon the subject of artificial feeding, in which he recognizes the fact, that it is an easy thing to raise a feeble child if you do not too much strengthen its food. Indeed he believes, in view of what he calls the degeneracy of the women of this age and country, that artificial food, made from the milk of another animal, may result " in uninterrupted health, with vigor and energy of the bodily functions." At first examination it seems absurd that nature should not be able to produce in the natural fountain, the supply of food and the kind of food most likely to carry life with its consumption. And it surely seems strange, that the parent with reasoning powers should be most likely to destroy her child with food. We have every reason to believe, if it were intended that the new-born should be fed on solid material, that they would have been furnished with the means to bite or tear: If grain were to be their proper diet, the means of grinding it would have been furnished. If starch, in any form, was

to be the best means of furnishing flesh and fat and
bone to them, their physiological functions would
have been prepared for the work. Mothers stare
when told that the artificial food is too strong. It is
true that there are cases, in which the preparations
of Liebig and Ridge and others are borne by the
child, and there are, doubtless, cases in which they
seem to thrive better upon them than upon that
which the mother has provided. But the cases are
exceptional, and death, in the course of the second
summer or fall, is more sure to be the result than in
children for whom food of a more nearly natural
character is provided.

We are frequently having healthful looking, fat
children pointed out to us, as the result of food which
the doctor has forbidden; children who are said
never to have had a sick day, although the parents
were warned that there was cerebral disturbance in
the coffee cup and death in the bean pot. And
there are many of us, also, who, after a single score
of years, can count mothers around us before whom
we avoid conversation on this subject, least we bring
up unpleasant memories of the past.

Examples are frequently brought forward of
children, who, from the earliest period of life, have
fed on cow's milk, almost pure, and have lived and
done well. For every such case I believe that any
gentleman, who keeps written records of his cases,
can show accounts of twenty who have died. The
stomach of the new child was not made to digest,
and cannot digest starch, nor muscle, nor the firm
casein of the cow or goat. The calf and the kid are

3

older than the human child at the hour when they are born.

And all milk is not the same milk. The earlier age at which it is drawn from the breast of goat, or cow, or woman, the less casein is to be found in it. In case of the woman, the percentage of casein in the solid constituents varied from sixteen at the beginning, to thirty-one at the close of four months' nursing; while the percentage of sugar ran down from forty-nine to thirty-six during the same time.* Even with this enormous increase to nearly double the amount of cheese, the woman's milk does not come up to that of the average cow, in the quantity of casein produced. And were it the fact that the two kinds of milk were exactly equal in the percentage of their constituents, it is an easy experiment, with a bit of rennet and a wineglassful of each for a specimen, to see that though by the addition of water they may be made equal in their amount of coagulable matter, the character of the two masses is absolutely different. The milk of woman, with whatever it be curdled, forms its coagulum in smaller flakes, soft, and easily broken down; that of the cow is in solid masses, like the factory cheese, of which it is a specimen.

Fresh milk, as received by us in cities, in the summer, often becomes sour in the course of twenty-four hours, even when kept upon ice; and I am informed that upon the farm this is sometimes the case. The addition of bicarbonate of potash to the

* Note C.

milk, as soon as it is received, not only prevents its becoming acid, but also prevents the formation of such firm curd in the stomach, as would otherwise be the case. If milk, to which this salt has been added, be rejected by early vomiting, as is generally the case with a very young child, whose stomach is over distended, the curd will be found to resemble the softer curd formed from human milk.*

I am not chemist enough to detail the differences in organic masses bearing the same name, but any gentleman will find an interest in repeating the experiment himself. Addition of water to the milk of the cow does not alone sufficiently humanize it. The addition of cane sugar as a substitute for milk sugar, which human milk contains more largely than cow's milk, does not add much to the digestibility of the latter. That the child generally does better with pure crystallized cane sugar, than without any sugar added to its artificial food, there is no doubt: but it is not a perfect substitute for sugar of milk, often becoming vinegar in the stomach, and aggravating the sorrows of the infant dyspeptic. On the other hand, the sugar of milk is more likely to be properly digested, and, should lactic acid be the result, it is less likely to disagree.†

All cows are not alike. The boasted " one cow's milk " does not help the matter. In examining the article of Prof. Simon upon the subject, one finds that in several analyses of cow's milk, the solid con-

---

* The amount of bicarbonate of potash should be about one-half grain to each fluid ounce of milk.

† Note D.

stituents varied from one hundred and thirty-nine to one hundred and forty-three parts in a thousand. The largest amount of casein in the solid ingredients was fifty and three tenths per cent., and the smallest was forty-eight per cent. And what do his reports show to be the difference between this and human milk? In numerous specimens of human milk, the maximum of solid constituents was one hundred and thirty-eight and six-tenths parts in a thousand, the minimum was eighty-six parts only. Of these solid constituents the amount of casein was thirty-two and six-tenths per cent., the other twenty-two and seven-tenths only.

The children in this family have more power to digest their food than the children in that family. The power of digestion varies like the power of assimilation, or of hearing, or of thought. There is as much variation in mammary glands as in stomachs; and the well developed breast and the fertile ovary may not exist in one and the same body. The woman who has numerous children may be unfit to nurse one; the woman who has had and can have but one child, I have known to nurse five in succession. It is hard to forbid a mother to nurse her own child, but nursing may be suicide to her— it may be homicide to the child. In several families in which the attempt has been made by mothers to nurse, the children have grown rapidly and apparently in perfect health up to a particular age, when death from convulsion during dentition has followed. Later children, fed by hired nurse or upon cow' milk, have grown less rapidly, but have passed year

beyond the age of the brothers and sisters, and are
still living beyond the age of puberty. The woman
who has no milk is anxious to find one who has milk
but no child. Another woman, under similar circumstances, is jealous of the nurse, and anxious, as early
as possible, to change the food.

Single cases may be brought forward in abundance
to prove anything; and 1 wish to call attention to
the absurdity of binding ourselves by any one set of
observations.

Mrs. A. was unable to nurse her child, and a wet
nurse was obtained for it, upon whose milk it throve
well. Mrs. B. was unable to nurse her child. It
was put upon cow's milk, and that child did equally
well. Both were well cared for in every way.
Mrs. C. was unable to nurse her child, and it was fed
upon pap and early upon meat and vegetables, and
that apparently did as well as the other two. Mrs.
D.'s died on the breast; Mrs. E.'s child, on the bottle;
Mrs. F.'s child, on the mixed diet; and all of these
were equally neglected in every other way. This is
a fair pattern of the evidence usually brought forward to prove some point in medical and medicinal
treatment.

Notwithstanding the interesting paper by Dr.
Putnam last year, and which, I trust, he will follow
up by other experiments, I put aside altogether the
question of vegetable food for the new born child,
believing that the nearer to the human mammary
secretion the food can be made, the better.

It is indeed sometimes difficult to advise whether
the nourishment shall come from the woman or the

cow. On the whole, after considering all the points
that occur to me, and including among them, that
in my own field of observation the question is between the milk of woman and milkman's milk, I
have of late been inclined to feel that if the mother
herself cannot nurse, the chances of life are better
with the milk of the cow than with the milk and
neglect and deceit of the ordinary wet nurse. Its
being with us a mixture of milks is not of so much
consequence as the quality of the mixture.* But
the cow keeps good hours. She is not overworked
bodily, nor are her mental trials sufficient, after the
calf has been fairly removed, to trouble any of her
secretions. She has a comfortable home, and her
owner's profit demands that she shall be well cared
for. It is true, on the other hand, that farmers, like
other people, have their peculiar notions about the
treatment of stock ; and it is equally true that they
will allow nothing to be done which they suspect to
be injurious to the animal ; while the human nurse
will sometimes bolt the most indigestible of food,
with the confidence that Mrs. Winslow's Syrup, or
some other morphia preparation, will stop the child's
belly-ache and give her a night's rest.

Still the nurse may be kept on too strict a diet. It
occasionally makes one smile to find that the child
has been fed with arrow-root or oatmeal to-day,
because the nurse imprudently ate a piece of boiled
beet or cabbage yesterday, and that the consequence
was a restless night ; or that cow's milk was adopt-

---

* Note E.

ed for the day, " because vegetables were taken by
the nurse, and they always injure the milk." The
fact is, that carnivorous animals need flesh to make
their milk. You will find no sugar in the milk of the
bitch, and it is of no use to feed her as if it were
needed, Romulus and his brother to the contrary,
notwithstanding.* The graminivorous nurse needs
food fitted for her teeth, and upon any other, neither
she nor the offspring will do so well.

For the human nurse, a mixed diet is that pointed
out by reason and experience; and it is no more fair
to attribute the baby's green discharge to the use of
a digestible vegetable, leaving out of sight the mixture of ice cream, oysters, fruit cake and lobster
salad, after the sweating of last night's polka, than
it would be to conceal the fact that your cow was
stoned and beaten about the field yesterday, and fed
on hot slops at night, if she and the calf are both
sick to-day.

Beef and potatoes will make good milk, but an
alternation of these with mutton or fish,† with
squash or other vegetables and fruits, will keep the
patient in better health, and better milk will be the
result.

There is every reason for new experiment upon
the feeding both of nurses and children. We
take too much of the statements of the past upon
trust. Ale and porter, it is said by some, are good
articles to give to the nurse. Others will tell you

* Note F.
† There is a common but erroneous idea prevalent among women, that fish
is an article of food fatal in its effect upon recent nurses.

as surely, that they will eventually dry up the breast.
And many farmers tell you that apples will dry up
the milk of the cow.   An article in the *Hartford
Courant*, of this last season, gives an interesting
series of experiments by Mr. Erastus Ellsworth, of
East Windsor, Conn., upon this point.*   It surely
contains statements which are worth investigating;
and it is by no means uncertain that a similar set of
experiments may not show that the human nurse
may sometimes benefit by the same treatment with
fruit.   The writer says : " The popular notion that
apples lessen the flow of milk, seemed to have no
support except from the occasional breaking of
bounds by cattle pent from the orchard.   A glut of
apples, from piles gathered for the cider-mill, may
be as dangerous to an animal as a glut of grain or
green clover, and no more so.   Accordingly, a trial
of the abundance of windfalls, principally Greenings
and Baldwins, was commenced about August 1.   In
the manifold stomachs of a cow, these hard, sour
apples, when bruised and ground, become sweet and
soft quite as readily as in the vat of a cider-mill.   A
large cow, something along in years, feeding exclu-
sively in her summer pasture and producing four
wine quarts daily, was for the first experiment,
beginning with four quarts of apples night and
morning.   The quantity was increased, until at the
end of a week she was eating a bushel of the hard-
est, sourest windfall apples each day.   This cow was
near her time of going dry, but such was the effect

---

* A letter from Mr. Ellsworth to myself, a portion of which is at the close of
this paper, confirms the statement.   See Note G.

of the apples as to bring her produce of milk from four to rather more than six quarts per diem.

"Another cow, in fresher milk, yielding eight quarts daily, was then put upon a ration of apples. At this time of measurement, Mr. Ellsworth's cows had been running several days in rowen feed, which would naturally help to flush the milk-pail. Yet upon top of this succulent pasture the second cow was brought, when upon her full ration of apples — a half bushel, night and morning — to a regular daily yield of twelve to fourteen quarts of milk. * * * There arose a cry from the dairy, directly, for more milk-pans, and as the average increase upon the five cows was fully fifty per cent., and a notorious matter in the household, the warnings of ruin to Mr. Ellsworth's dairy from kind-hearted neighbors soon ceased. The butter made from this milk was first-rate, as I had an opportunity of knowing. I inquired particularly whether at any time there had been the least symptom of ill effect upon the cow — upon the bowels or kidneys. 'Nothing of the sort, sir.' * * * He told me he was eighty-three years old—coming gloriously to the fore with these timely, painstaking and exact experiments, while young farmers, routine farmers, close farmers, men who wouldn't waste a cent's worth if they knew it, are actually gathering apples from their fall seeding grounds, and dumping them into holes in the street, rather than risk giving them to their cattle."

Undoubtedly every one has seen the milk of some nurse disturbed by the food which another could take with advantage. This surely is not remarkable,

4

when we remember that one of us is distressed by
eating beef fat, while he can swallow mutton fat
without stint; that one can eat oysters, but has
cholera morbus after clams; that cocoanut causes
no distress to this patient, while strawberries produce
erythema in that one; and even the smell of the
lobster wheelbarrow is followed by asthma and
urticaria in the very patient who can make a supper
of olives and cheese with ice cream and coffee, pass
a quiet night and wake in the morning with an
appetite for breakfast.

People are equally prejudiced upon the subject of
one cow's milk. But it is as necessary to know about
the cow as about any other of your domestics. It
is not needful that one cow should furnish the whole
supply, and those gentlemen who praise the con-
densed milk as a substitute for it, without any
reservation, do not seem to understand that each can
has in it the remnants of milk from fifty cows, and
perhaps from fifty different cows in each new can.

The fact that the milk is from a new milch cow
proves nothing in its favor. There is as much
difference in recent nurses as in old ones. The
questions are: Is the milk good? Does this milk
contain all that is needed for this child? Does it
contain anything injurious to this child which can be
got rid of? The special advantage to be obtained
from milk from the new milch cow consists in its
being less caseous than human milk, and in its
bearing the same relation to the milk of later date,
that the human colostrum does.

I. A writer in the *American Agriculturist*, in

October, 1870 (and his remarks will apply to human nurses also), says: "We may divide cows into two extreme classes with regard to the quality of the milk. One class gives milk; the other, milk and water: while if we have reference to the quantity of milk given, we find almost as great a difference in the one class as the other. The milk of those which give enormous quantities, say twenty-five to thirty quarts a day, is rarely very rich; ten to twelve per cent. of cream being almost as much as we have ever known the milk of such cows to yield. In some cases it is extremely poor, yielding four per cent. or even less. It is not only among the enormous milkers that we find the milk-and-water class of cows: there are thousands in the country, valued by their owners as excellent milkers, which really yield only milk and water, and very thin at that. The milk is mixed with that of others at the time of straining, and the good wife never dreams that some poor, thin, bony, hungry cow that gives only eight quarts of milk at her best, is producing a pound and a half to two pounds of butter a day, while the favorite of the herd, a whole or three-quarters Durham, that gives twelve quarts at a milking, does not add four pounds of butter a week to the family stores: yet it is true in many cases."

Now, for the human child, it is not needful that the milk should be the richest in butter. That is the most variable of all the constituents in human milk, even in milk upon which children are doing the best.* Possibly that which would be the poorest

---

* Note H.

for the dairy, might be the best for the child. Experiment alone can answer that question, and decide what good milk is.

"However much," says Simon, "the nutriment of the mother may vary, no great influence is thereby exerted on the relative quantities of casein and sugar. The changes consist in a greater or less degree of saturation, in the rich yellowish white or the bluish color, in the quantity of the milk and in the amount of solid constituents ; with the exception of the variation in quantity, all the other changes are dependent on an increase or diminution of the butter; the former occurs under the use of a copious and nutritious diet, the latter when the food is poor and scanty."

He says that he analyzed the milk of a very poor woman fifteen times, at regular intervals during half a year, beginning on the second day after delivery. She was suddenly deprived of the means of obtaining the ordinary necessaries of life. At this time her food was sufficiently abundant (Nov. 11), but containing only eight and six-tenths per cent. of solid material. On the 18th of November she was placed on full and nutritious meat diet. The milk consequently ran from the breast copiously, and left eleven and nine-tenths per cent. of solid constituents. She again became destitute, and while in this condition, Dec. 1, the milk again became very thin, and left only nine and eight-tenths of solid constituents. On January 4, after she had been supplied for two days with a nutritious meat diet, the milk was very rich in solids, which amounted to twelve and six-tenths per cent.*

II. Cow's milk does not contain all that is neces-sary for the human child. The proportion of sugar, not cane, but milk sugar, is much less than it should be; and although the cane sugar may be to a certain extent a substitute, it is no more a proper substitute than lard would be for butter, provided indeed the substitution could be made. Many may endure it and be better than without any sugar; but it will not be perfect in its effect. If it becomes acid it is not lactic acid but vinegar that is formed; and where the one may do service, the other will surely do harm.†

III. Does it contain anything injurious to the child? The statements before made, concerning the hard, caseous masses, is answer sufficient. If the child's stomach has not been tampered with by drugs, or by attempts to force diet more nutritious than is required, it will digest cow's milk, properly prepared. And the physician who means success must bear in mind that he is to take the whole responsibility of the case, even if it obliges him to be cook as well. Conscious that change for the better cannot always be immediate, he must be prepared to meet doubts and answer questions. The result, if he is fair and open in his course, will show that he is right. The discharges of the child must all be seen. He must be able to distinguish colors, and must know that large stains of uric acid are not blood.

---

* Note I.   † Note K.

The first experiment to try, is the removing a portion of the casein, by allowing the milk to settle, and watering the top. This gives us more butter and less casein at the top. This is to be watered and sweetened for use. With many, even new-born children, this diet will answer. With many other children, pain follows this food also, and the discharges are still undigested curd. Just so long as undigested food passes from the bowels of adult or child, that particular article should be diminished in quantity or rejected altogether, or possibly you may diminish the amount at one feeding and repeat the feeding oftener.* Milk which passes from the rectum in form of curd, is, of course, of no use. The curd is just so much food wasted or thrown away. You may think the milk too absurdly diluted, but it is still the fact, that what passes in form of curd is of no use. If your child continues to grow in weight, however slowly, and seems well in every way, what harm in feeding it on milk and water, one part in a hundred even, more especially if sickness, indigestion and pain follow the change of proportion to one in fifty.

A great quantity of urine, perhaps, is passed by children fed on milk largely diluted, with great inconvenience to the mother. The inconvenience to the child, however, is less than pain would be.

But you may reduce the proportion of milk in some cases to only a tenth of the mixture, and still

* This proposition, recently re-published by Dr. Brown-Sequard, and by many supposed to be his original proposition, has been practised many years by physicians in this vicinity.

undigested casein and pain are the immediate consequence; diarrhœa and waste, with mesenteric disease
or fatal convulsion, the ultimate result.   Drugs in
such patients are useless.   Calomel may blacken the
discharges, rhubarb may turn them to an orange
color ; but these will not cure indigestion.   Opium
may relieve pain, but it will not increase the natural
power of the child's stomach.   In getting rid of the
casein, you may do all that is needed ; but remember
that in getting rid of that you have done more.   You
have thrown away also, in like proportion, the
butter, the natural sugar and the salts.*   You may
not only have removed an enemy, but with him some
of the friends.   Before allowing matters to proceed
to that extremity, it would be well to use rennet, or
one of its preparations, and remove a large proportion of the casein with as small an amount of the
other constituents as possible.

Remembering, however, the feeble condition of
your patient, continue to add water to the whey you
have made, until the discharges contain no more
undigested cheese.

Gentlemen will be surprised to find how much
caseous matter will continue to pass the bowels,
after they are positive that all has been removed
from the ingesta.   I have known the whey reduced
by adding seven and eight parts of water to one,
before the digestion became relieved, and the child
could take food without suffering.

But how long is the child to go on in this manner?
Just so long as he fails to digest his food prepared

---

* Note L.

in any other way. Each case must be judged by
itself.   The strength of food should be slowly
increased, and when pain or curd follows its increase,
dilute again, and wait a little longer.*

And this leads to another point. As the child
grows older, it is true that it needs older food. But
when should the change be made? Not while it is
doing perfectly well. Not when the irritation of a
new tooth is going on. It should be when the system
is undisturbed. If the change be made while the
growth is progressive, it is well to be cautious not
to force the change too rapidly. Under such circumstances we often find food pass undigested,
diarrhœa and vomiting supervene, and it is often
impossible to return successfully to the original diet.

Remembering the great disturbance of the system
at every change of habit and of life, bear also in
mind that an increase of food and a reduction in the
length of dress should not come together. The
impending irruption of a tooth is sufficient reason for
delay. Teething is not a disease, but whether it be
at six months or at six or eighteen years, the coming
of a tooth has placed your charge's system in such
condition that he wavers between health and disease,
and possibly a very slight change in diet may settle
the question of life or death. So long as the fonta-
nelle is not depressed, unless hydrocephalus exist,
the child is not starving. So long as, from week to
week, there is no loss of weight, the child is not
starving. So long as it is not starving, with watch-

* Note M.

fulness you can be a little longer in carrying on the
experiment. But suppose it be starving, and is, at
the same moment, passing its food undigested, and
wearing itself out with fretfulness and pain, what is
to be gained by the addition of more food, which
cannot be assimilated, and which is only going to
increase the suffering? The want of sufficient and
proper clothing, more especially in a cold climate,
or in an excessively changeable climate, as that of
Massachusetts is, even in the summer season, helps
to explain the large number of deaths among children. This is true, whether the last cause of death
be in the brain, the thorax, or digestive canal. The
more likely seat of trouble is in the latter. The
summer is looked upon by mothers as the more
dangerous for children before completion of the first
dentition ; but, except in filthy localities, they will
find that there are no more deaths among them from
abdominal troubles in summer, than from thoracic
diseases in the winter. There is, however, a mixed
season of heat and cold, the period of hot days and
chilly nights, in September and October, when, in
the first few hours in the morning, more clothing is
needed than at midday, when diarrhœa, dysentery
and cholera infantum make their severest ravages.
It is at this season of the year when the children
between one and three years old, who have not
completed their dentition, become the victims of too
early weaning. There is a very common opinion
that children run great risks if weaned in the
months of May, June, or July. Other things being
equal, the older a child in good health is, at the time

5

of weaning, the better is its chance for life.   Under no circumstances should a change from the breast to stronger diet be made while a tooth is pressing upon the gum.

Whether the pregnancy of the mother nurse requires that the child should be taken from the breast, is a question which generally is settled without calling upon the doctor.   If the milk does not become suppressed, which is sometimes the case, it is more likely that the unborn child rather than the nursling will suffer.   I have known four children in succession to be nursed by the mother without knowing when her pregnancy was to close, and have seen a contest between the child of five years with the child of two for a chance at the same nipple. If they have been removed from the breast prematurely, you cannot teach them to nurse, nor if they have been taught to eat food fit only for adults, can you by any drugging make their stomachs recover the tone which the ignorance of the parents has allowed to be destroyed.   The little white, sugary powder of calomel, left by the one who pretends to believe in homœopathy, under the name of arsenicum; the more honest, but equally dangerous dark powder of hydrargyrum cum cretâ; the nearly tasteless white powder of sugar with a little morphia, under the name of bryonia or nux; or the unmistakeable chalk mixture of the pharmacopœia, are all drugs.   But the best medicine is an extra yard or two of flannel applied externally ; an additional foot of clothing at the bottom of the dress, and a few inches more at the top, are better than rhubarb or opium.   The case is rare in which anything but rest will check the vomiting in the choleraic class of cases, and the strong craving for simple cold water, if indulged to the fullest possible extent, will often relieve the suffering, which is sure to be increased by the sips and spoonfuls which only aggravate.

Fashion, at this moment, has begun to indulge the new-born child in a sufficient amount of clothing, and, for a few years, it will not probably be necessary to preach in favor of the high-necked and long-sleeved dress. But when fashion changes, and the open neck and exposed breast are again in vogue, it will be the easiest matter in the world for the majority of young mothers to convince themselves that children can be toughened to endure the cold, and that health and long life will probably be produced by exposure.

Still the teachings of medical thermometry may avail somewhat, and it may be possible to convince the world that, although children produce heat rapidly, they also part with it rapidly; just as the stove which is well protected in the house will, with the same amount of fuel, keep warm longer than one which is exposed out of doors.

Cleanliness is next to Godliness. But some very good and healthy people are very dirty; and making clean the outside of the dish does not argue, with any certainty, the good condition of what is within. But apparent cleanliness may be urged too far. So long as the new-born child is blue from want of properly inflated lungs, and the consequent want of proper action of the heart, it is certainly possible that it may be supplied with too much external heat.* Heat and suffocation more surely go hand in hand than dyspnœa with a cold skin. The cold may produce a cry and an inflation of lung, that nothing else will. The respiration once established, the skin once reddened and the extremities once warmed, the return of lividity is much to be deprecated; although if the child be strong and hearty, he may fight through all exposure and come off conqueror.

Children may be washed too much. The feeble, chilly child is often a sacrifice upon the altar of Hygeia. Dirt is, to some extent, a conventional matter. What its character is to be considered, depends very much upon the position of an article. The odor of the rose would add nothing pleasant to the flavor of roasted beef, nor would tobacco smoke to the cologne bottle. Soap is no fit dressing for bread, nor the sweetest of oils for a cambric pocket handkerchief. But a child may be as clean with the application of oil as of soap. Indeed, the one who has tried to remove the vernix caseosa with soap and water alone, knows that it cannot be done at one washing. The previous use of oil upon the skin is almost a necessity. The use of oil alone, at a first dressing, is not a dirty practice. The child may be made cleaner by it than with soap and water alone, and if its circulation is at all imperfect after the first washing, it will be more comfortable to be washed with oil alone than with any combination. But it is after the first cleansing that an oil, not

* See W. F. Edwards on the Influence of Physical Agents upon Life.

become rancid, is often a useful application, and
therefore not a dirty one.   The oil, externally, pro-
motes heat within.   There are many adults to whom
I could point, who never knew what it was to sleep
with warm feet, even with stockings upon them,
until they were advised greasing the legs and feet at
bedtime.   No one would suppose, from any appear-
ance of oiliness, that that had been used for the
child in place of water.   If it be needed, the skin
takes up a very large proportion of it, and there is
no more reason why the child's clothing should be
soiled by the remainder, than for its being soiled
with water upon the skin after an ordinary wash.
The towel, in either case, should do its portion of
the work.   Many a feeble child has taken up oil
enough by the skin to keep it alive for weeks, as
many a phthisical patient has been oiled with the
result of less cough, more quiet sleep, and an actual
gain of weight.   If any article, used externally
upon the child, makes it more likely to take cold, as
it is called, or do it an injury, it is the wasteful use
of brandy or rum, which dissolves the oil from the
skin, and drying it, throws extra work upon the
lungs and heart.

One more combination of the enemies standing
more especially in the way of infantile life, is the
drug bottle and the popular treatise.   The shrewd
trickster, who calls himself homœopath, has the
advantage of us here.   The little sugar pills, to be
dissolved in so much water and given by the tea-
spoonful, the mother will tell you are excellent for
children.   Before she used those, it was necessary

to send for the doctor in the night; but now, with a minute fraction of the pill, the child goes to sleep much better than when she gave it paregoric; and it wakes up well in the morning. But why not learn from quacks? A placebo is a medicine as much as hysteria is a disease. You can kill a man equally, whether you scare him to death with the warm water which he thinks is blood running over his skin, or blow him from a cannon's mouth. The one makes less noise, perhaps, than the other. Those of us who realize that we are fighting under the banner upon which the motto is *"naturâ duce,"* and who are growing more numerous each year, are perfectly willing to use the placebo, where placebo is the proper medicine. But we are not willing to enrol ourselves in that contemptible army of knaves, who, from fear of not getting patients enough, can say to the mother: "I practise in either way"; and who whispers to himself, " you pays your money and you has your choice." If he need drugging, do the work, but do it honorably and openly. Let the patient alone who does not need treatment.

There is a penny wise and pound foolish way, in many families, of consulting popular treatises on medicinal treatment; and the more the mother reads, the more doubtful she grows, the more miserable the infant becomes, the more frequently the treatment is changed, the more the necessity arises of sending for the doctor. Oh! the misery, when sick, of knowing anything of ourselves; the misfortune of ever having heard of ulcerated Peyer's patches, of having the knowledge that one has a lung, a stomach, a pancreas, a pineal gland; the suffering from the recollection of how little chloral hydrate killed one man, and the memory of Christison's statement of the very small dose of opium that was fatal in a particular case! And is it strange that, since Buchan is out of date, and the more modern treatise is to be frequently found on the sitting-room table, bearing a surname which so many of us early learned to respect, and which is supposed by many of the public to be his work; is it strange, in the confused and pictorially illustrated medley of no less than three systems of medicinal treatment, that the poor and ignorant mother, who wishes to save expense, hurries her nursing child into its coffin?

The day may be approaching when popular treatises upon medicine and physiology will be of occasional value; but I doubt whether they will ever be of any more service to the world than popular treatises upon watch-making or the building of locomotives. It may be that some ignorant neighbor's prescription may be lived through, and some tough child may escape the normal consequences of a cold bath administered according to popular rules.

The case is by no means unknown, in which a shot through the head did not destroy the intellect; and a bullet through the chest has been followed only by a bloody expectoration. The evidence in favor of popular treatises upon medicine, is equally strong with that upon the harmlessness of bullets. And the evidence amounts to this, they do not always kill.

NOTES.

NOTE A. — Page 3.

THE number of charter members of the Society was thirty-one. Twenty of these were graduates of Harvard University, but I can only find that ten of them ever received either the degree of Bachelor or Doctor of Medicine. The earliest graduate of the college was John Sprague, of the class of 1730; who, fifty-one years later, was sufficiently interested in the objects of the Society to petition for its charter. For many years after the organization was completed, the names of officers and members are recorded as M.D., M.B., A.M., Hon., Esq., or plain Dr. There are very few of the first two, till after the year 1800.

It may be interesting, as a simple matter of history, to point to some of the early and honorable names:

EDWARD AUGUSTUS HOLYOKE, our first president in 1781, was not M.D. till 1783.

The first secretary, Dr. NATHANIEL WALKER APPLETON, never was M.D.

SAMUEL DANFORTH, an original member, and president in 1795, became M.D. nine years after joining.

JOSHUA FISHER, president; was not M.D. till 1804, several years later.

WILLIAM KNEELAND, president in 1784, never had the degree.

ISAAC RAND, an original member, president in 1797, at which time he was Master of Arts only, received the degree of M.D. two years later.

COTTON TUFTS, an original member, graduate of the college in 1749, was not M.D. till 1785, and became president in 1787.

6

JOHN WARREN, an original member, and instrumental in founding the medical department of the University, received his M.D. in 1786, and became president in 1804.

JOHN BROOKS, who was a Colonel in the army of the revolution, Governor of the Commonwealth and President of this Society, received the honorary degree of M.D. as late as 1810, and twenty-three years after being made a Master of Arts.

WILLIAM EUSTIS, who was a General in the army, and afterwards Secretary-of-War and Governor of the Commonwealth, never received the degree, although a member of this Society.

It is not, at this day, a requisite that one shall be M.D., to enable him to obtain admission, but that he shall be sufficiently well fitted in certain branches to enable him to pass a satisfactory examination.

NOTE B. — Page 8.

"The curious fact has occurred that maize, or Indian corn, was raised so plentifully in some of the western States the last year, and commanded so low a price, that it was largely used as fuel ; it having been found that a ton of corn is equal to a cord of wood for heating purposes, and did not cost so much by three dollars.—*Am. Hist. Record, April,* 1873, *p.* 188.

NOTE C. — Page 18.

Having spoken of the use of cow's milk as a substitute for that of the human female, and, indeed, as often preferable to that of the hired nurse, I do not forget the great adulteration to which it is often subjected in our larger cities. Neither do I forget that, in such places, much of it comes scores of miles, and is sometimes several days old before it reaches its destination. Indeed, no milk delivered from out of town, at a moderately early hour, can come from the cow on the day of delivery. While one person is in town, distributing milk, another is engaged out of town, collecting the milk for to-morrow's supply. He gets a gallon here and there, or five or ten gallons at another place, until his rounds are made. This milk is put in large cans in a cool place until night, when a portion is poured off for cream, and the rest is brought up as nearly as possible to the standard by the addition of salt, coloring matters, &c. The report of Dr. Arthur H. Nichols and Prof. F. Babcock, in the last Report of the

State Board of Health, contains some interesting information upon the subject of the adulterations. It is more than probable that no absolutely pure milk is brought to the city of Boston. From my own observations, I do not believe that the milk supplied by the so-called Milk Consumers' Association is so good as that supplied by many milkmen. The reason for this is, perhaps, to be found in the union with the Association of those who were interested in making it unpopular.

With all these facts prominently before me, living in this city, I should prefer cow's milk for children to arrowroot, Liebig's food, Ridge's food, groats, or any vegetable food, and to the milk of most wet nurses.

Note D. — Page 19.

The following statement I received from Prof. E. S. Wood, M.D., of Harvard University :—

"The first action of the stomach upon all kinds of sugar is the same, viz. : the conversion into glucose or grape sugar, which conversion is, however, due to the action of the saliva, or pancreatic fluid in the intestine. Sugar of milk *as such* is never found in the system except in the milk contained in the lacteal glands, the cells of which, therefore, have the property of reconverting glucose to milk sugar.

Cane sugar never becomes converted into milk sugar by the action of the stomach, but into glucose. Milk sugar when pure is not susceptible of fermentation, but when in contact with casein, as in milk, it undergoes fermentation and lactic acid is formed, and small amounts of butyric acid, also, if the fermentation proceed far enough. This change may take place in the alimentary canal if digestion be impeded, so that the casein and milk sugar remain in contact sufficiently long for fermentation to take place. Cane sugar will also undergo this same variety of fermentation if its solution be added to casein or old cheese. In lactic fermentation, no alcohol is produced.

Milk sugar has no effect upon the process of digestion, unless that process be an impaired one, in which case the acid produced, as well as the other products of the decomposition which would be formed, might irritate a little and create still more disturbance of digestion, in the same manner as undigested food always does."

NOTE E. — Page 22.

The County of Suffolk is to a larger extent supplied with milkman's milk than any other county in the Commonwealth. As no milk is raised within its borders, it is probable that none, absolutely free from additions, is supplied to consumers. Under such circumstances we should naturally suppose that more of its children fall victims to cholera infantum. It is the fact, however, that Suffolk County stands in the fifth place on the list for the year 1870. The whole number of deaths of children of two years and under, for the year 1870, was 8,151 ; of which 1,914 were by cholera infantum, or 0.234 per cent. Suffolk County, as may be seen, stood a trifle below the average.

The order of fatality, by counties, was as follows :—

	Deaths at two years old and less.	Per cent. by Cholera Infantum.
Middlesex,	1,606	0.286
Hampshire,	181	0.265
Worcester,	1,056	0.254
Essex,	978	0.234
Suffolk,	2,310	0.230
Norfolk,	366	0.218
Hampden,	437	0.215
Franklin,	114	0.201
Plymouth,	218	0.183
Bristol,	526	0.161
Barnstable,	81	0.160
Berkshire,	264	0.151
Dukes and Nantucket,	14	0.071

NOTE F. — Page 23.

The milk was drawn from one of the teats which was not used by the pup ; it was very thick (whereas from the teats which the pup was in the habit of sucking, it was very thin), had a disagreeable animal odor, and a rather saltish, mawkish, but not sweet taste. A period of ten days elapsed between the two analyses.

	1st.	2nd.
Water,	657.4	682.0
Solid constituents,	342.6	318.0
Butter,	162.0	133.0
Casein,	174.0	146.0
Extractive matter and traces of sugar,	29.0	30.0
Fixed salts,	15.0	14.8

Simon (Sydenham Soc. Edit., vol. ii. p. 66).

It is worth while to compare the enormous amount of casein and butter in these two cases, and also the amount of sugar with that in the milk of the woman and cow. Taking Simon's analyses of the milk of the three species, they stand, in a thousand parts, as follows :

	WOMAN.		COW.		BITCH.	
Butter	54.0	8.0	40.0	38.0	162.0	133.0
Casein	45.2	19.6	72.0	68.0	174.0	146.0
Sugar	62.4	39.2	28.0	29.0	Traces of Sugar.	

The milk of other animals was also examined by Simon [vide Sydenham Soc. Edit., p. 61 et seq.], and in a thousand parts we find that they contain :

	ASS.			GOAT.		EWE.	
Butter	12.10	12.9	1.1	45.6	29.9	58.0	42.0
Casein	16.74	19.5	18.2	91.2	52.9	153.0	45.0
Sugar	62.31	62.9	60.8	43.8	20.7	42.0	50.0

With the exception of the woman's milk, and that from the cow, he quotes his record from other chemists.

Note G. — Page 24.

E. Windsor Hill, Conn., April 24, 1873.

Charles E. Buckingham, M.D.

Dear Sir:—The correspondent of the *Courant* called on me for information respecting an experiment which I was making in regard to feeding apples to cows, and I gave him verbally the information which he published. When his article appeared, I regarded it as correct, and giving a true statement of all the important facts. I fed at that time about two hundred (200) bushels to my cows and other cattle, with great satisfaction to myself; and could add, if necessary, to prove that there is great profit in the business, when contrasted with the miserable practice of converting apples into brandy.

The business requires care and strict attention to the following directions :—Commence giving the cow half a peck

at a time, twice a day, and add gradually to the quantity for
eight or ten days, till the quantity reaches half a bushel at a
time, say one bushel per day, given morning and evening. I
would in no case exceed that quantity for the largest cows.
To the smaller cows, I would not give so much, but say ½ to
¾ bushel. Reason for this rule—if cows have free access to
all they will eat, they will make themselves sick and dry up
their milk. This has happened so often in years past, that a
great prejudice exists against feeding apples.

I place my cows in the stable, where each is confined to her
own allowance, and for fear of getting choked, chop the
apples. This helps the cow to eat those which are hard. I
have never had a creature get choked, but think the practice
a good precaution. Some cows will show the effect more
than others. After all the attention I gave the matter, I judged
the effect was to increase the flow of milk from two to four
quarts daily.

Only one instance occurred in which I had occasion to
discontinue the feed, and that was a yoke of working oxen;
my *men thought* the apples scoured them.

If you think that I may furnish any additional information,
please write for it.   *   *   *   *   *   *   *

Yours in haste,

Very respectfully,

E. ELLSWORTH.

NOTE II. — Page 27.

Referring again to Simon's observations [Sydenham Soc.
Edit., p. 51 et seq.], we find no ingredient more variable than
the butter. The first is the average of fourteen analyses,
made at different periods with the milk of the same woman;
second, the milk of a woman aged thirty-six years; third, of
a nurse aged twenty years; fourth, the maxima, and fifth,
the minima of numerous analyses. The sixth, seventh and
eighth (quoted from Clem) were made on the fourth, ninth
and twelfth days, respectively, after delivery. From the
ninth to the fourteenth, inclusive, quoted from L'Heretier;
the fifteenth and sixteenth, from Haidlen.

1.	2.	3.	4.	5.	6.	7.	8.
25.3	38.0	28.8	54.0	8.0	42.9	35.3	33.4

9.	10.	11.	12.	13.	14.	15.	16.
42.5	52.0	35.5	40.5	54.8	56.3	13.0	34.0

Note I. — Page 29.

The following are the results of fourteen analyses made by Simon, and which are alluded to in the text; the dates there alluded to are in italics.

	Spec. Grav.	Water.	Solids.	Casein.	Sugar.	Butter.	Fixed Salts.
Aug. 31.	1031.6	873.2	126.8	21.2	62.4	34.6	0.84
Sept. 7.	1030.0	883.8	116.2	19.6	57.6	31.4	1.66
8.	1030.0	899.0	101.0	25.7	52.3	18.0	2.00
14.	1030.0	883.6	116.4	22.0	52.0	26.4	1.78
Oct. 27.	1034.0	898.2	101.8	43.0	45.0	14.0	2.74
Nov. 3.	1032.0	886.0	114.0	45.2	39.2	27.4	2.87
Nov. 11.	1034.5	914.0	86.0	35.3	39.5	8.0	2.40
Nov. 18.	1033.0	880.6	119.4	37.0	45.4	34.0	2.50
25.	1033.4	890.4	109.6	38.5	47.5	19.0	2.70
Dec. 1.	1032.0	902.0	98.0	39.0	49.0	8.0	2.08
8.	1033.0	890.0	110.0	41.0	43.0	22.0	2.76
16.	1034.4	891.0	109.0	42.0	44.0	20.0	2.68
31.	1034.0	861.4	138.6	31.0	52.0	54.0	2.35
Jan. 4.	1032.0	873.6	126.4	40.0	46.0	37.0	2.70

They show at a glance "that, with few exceptions, first, the quantity of casein is at its minimum at the commencement; it then rises considerably, and ultimately attains a nearly fixed proportion; that, second, the quantity of sugar is at its maximum at the commencement, and subsequently diminishes; and that, third, the butter is a very variable constituent of the milk."

Note K. — Page 29.

See Professor Wood's letter in Note D.

Note L. — Page 31.

The proportion of fixed salts appears to be greater in the lower animals than in the woman; the largest percentage in the healthy woman that I can find, being 4.5, in the cow 6.77, and in the bitch 15.0.

Note M. — Page 32.

The following schedule, prepared by Dr. Cumming, is worthy the experiment of every one who has the charge of children's food. For myself, I have never failed to find it satisfactory.

"*Schedule showing the Dilution of Milk at various ages:*

For a child from	MILK.	WATER.	FOOD.
2 to 10 days old,	1¼ gills,	3¼ gills,	making 4½ gills
10 to 20 " "	1¾ "	4¼ "	" 6 "
20 to 30 " "	2½ "	6 "	" 8½ "
1 to 1½ months,	3 "	6¾ "	" 9¾ "
1½ to 2 "	3½ "	7 "	" 10½ "
2 to 2½ "	4 "	7½ "	" 11½ "
2½ to 3 "	4½ "	7½ "	" 12 "
3 to 3½ "	5 "	7½ "	" 12½ "
3½ to 4 "	5½ "	7½ "	" 13 "
4 to 4½ "	6 "	7½ "	" 13½ "
4½ to 5 "	6½ "	7½ "	" 14 "
5 to 6 "	7 "	7 "	" 14 "
6 to 7 "	7½ "	6½ "	" 14 "
7 to 8 "	8 "	6 "	" 14 "
8 to 0 "	8¼ "	6 "	" 14¼ "
9 to 10 "	8½ "	6 "	" 14½ "
10 to 11 "	8¾ "	6 "	" 14¾ "
11 to 12 "	9 "	5½ "	" 14½ "
12 to 15 "	0½ "	5¼ "	" 14¾ "
15 to 18 "	9½ "	5 "	" 14½ "
18 onward "	10 "	5 "	" 15 "

"It will be well to have a cup holding a gill when full. Eight ordinary table-spoonfuls equal one gill; six equal three quarters of a gill; four equal half a gill; and two equal a quarter of a gill."

www.ingramcontent.com/pod-product-compliance
Lightning Source LLC
Chambersburg PA
CBHW021555270326
41931CB00009B/1223